The **Green** and **Hairy**
Joke Book

What do you get if you cross
a gooseberry with an elephant?
A pie that never forgets

What's green and hairy and flies
a UFO?
A Martian gooseberry

How do you make a gooseberry stew?
*By telling lots of green and hairy
jokes . . .*

The **Green** and **Hairy** Joke Book

Gus Berry
with cartoons by Tony Blundell

A Magnet Book

For Annabel

First published in Great Britain 1987
by Magnet Paperbacks
Michelin House, 81 Fulham Road, London SW3 6RB
Reprinted 1988 and 1989
Text copyright © 1987 Martyn Forester
Illustrations copyright © 1987 Tony Blundell
Photoset by 🅰 Tek Art Ltd, Croydon, Surrey
Printed in Great Britain
by Cox & Wyman Ltd, Reading

ISBN 0 416 97230 6

Knock, knock,
– *Who's there?*
Lettuce.
– *Lettuce who?*
Lettuce tell you
a few good green
and hairy jokes.

Customer: Have you any wild gooseberries?
Waiter: No sir, but we can take some ordinary ones and irritate them for you.

Should you eat gooseberries with your fingers?

No, fingers should be eaten separately.

Customer: Why is my piece of gooseberry pie all smashed?
Waiter: Well, you said 'Fetch a piece of gooseberry pie, and step on it.'

Bert: My dad went to pick some gooseberries last night, slipped, and broke his leg.

Fred: That's terrible. What did your mother do?

Bert: She opened a tin of peaches instead.

When do elephants paint their toe-nails green?

When they want to hide upside-down in a pot of gooseberry jam.

Man in restaurant: Will you join me in a piece of gooseberry pie?
Woman: Do you think there's room for both of us?

Man on train: Excuse me, I think you're sitting in my seat.
Woman: Can you prove it?
Man: I think so. You see, I left a big piece of gooseberry pie on it.

Why are gooseberry seeds like gateposts?

Because they propagate.

Why is a Boy Scout like a tin
of gooseberries?

They are both prepared.

What's green and smells?

Kermit's nose.

What's green and hairy and flies a UFO?

A Martian gooseberry.

What's green and hairy and takes aspirins?

A gooseberry with a headache.

What's green and hairy and coughs?

A gooseberry with a bad chest.

What's green and hairy and sits on the sea bed?

A gooseberry in a submarine.

What do you get if you cross
a gooseberry with a tiger?

*I don't know – but I wouldn't
try eating it!*

What do you call a gooseberry
who insults a farmer?

Fresh fruit.

What do you get if you cross a
gooseberry with an elephant?

A pie that never forgets.

What do you get if you cross a
gooseberry with an aeroplane?

Pie in the sky.

What do you get
if you cross a
gooseberry with
an alligator?

*A gooseberry
that bites back.*

What do you get if you cross two
gooseberries with a banana skin?

A pair of green slippers.

What do you get if you cross
a bowl of gooseberries with
a pair of roller skates?

Meals on wheels.

What do you get if you cross
a gooseberry with an elk?

Gooseberry mousse.

What do you get if you cross
a gooseberry with an idiot?

Gooseberry fool.

Two ants were in a supermarket. They climbed up on a shelf and on to a box containing a gooseberry pie. Suddenly the first ant began running.

'Wait for me!' cried the other ant. 'What's the hurry?'

'Can't you read?' said the first. 'It says here: TEAR ALONG THE DOTTED LINE.'

What is green and hairy and
extremely dangerous?

A herd of stampeding gooseberries.

How do you stop a herd of
stampeding gooseberries from
charging?

Take away their credit cards.

What do you get if you cross
the M1 with a gooseberry?

Run over.

What is green and bald outside,
and green and hairy inside?

An inside-out gooseberry.

What is red outside, green and
hairy inside, and very crowded?

A bus full of gooseberries.

Girl: Try some of this gooseberry tart
I've just made.
Boy: Ugh, it's awful!
Girl: You're wrong. It definitely says
in my cookery book that this recipe
is delicious.

Man in café: I don't like this gooseberry pie.

Woman cook: Well, I'll have you know I was making gooseberry pies before you were born.

Man: Perhaps this is one of them.

A tramp knocked on a door and asked the lady of the house for some food. 'Didn't I give you a slice of my home-made gooseberry tart a week ago?' she asked.

'Yes,' said the tramp, 'but I'm a lot better now.'

What's green
and hairy
and red
all over?

*An embarrassed
gooseberry.*

Teacher: How do you spell
'gooseberry'?
Pupil: G-u-z-b-r-y.
Teacher: The dictionary spells it
g-o-o-s-e-b-e-r-r-y.
Pupil: You didn't ask me how the
dictionary spells it!

Teacher: If I had forty gooseberries
in one hand,
and forty in
the other,
what would
I have?
Pupil: Big hands.

What did the dentist say when his wife baked a gooseberry pie?

'Can I do the filling?'

What's the difference between a gooseberry and an elephant?

A gooseberry is green.

*　　　　*　　　　*

What did Hannibal say when he saw the elephants coming?

'Here come the gooseberries' – he was colour-blind!

What's the difference between a gooseberry, a gorilla, and a tube of glue?
– *I don't know.*
Well, you can bite into a gooseberry, but you can't bite into a gorilla.
– *What about the tube of glue?*
I thought that was where you'd get stuck!

Why is a gooseberry green and hairy?

Because if it was white and bald, it would be a Mint Imperial.

What's blue and hairy?

A gooseberry holding its breath.

What did one gooseberry bush say
to the other gooseberry bush?

Take me to your weeder.

What did one gooseberry say to
the other gooseberry?

Nothing. Gooseberries can't talk.

What's the best thing to put into a
gooseberry pie?

Your teeth.

What's green and hairy and
wears sunglasses?

A gooseberry on holiday.

What is a gooseberry's skin
most used for?

To keep the gooseberry together.

How do you stop a gooseberry
ripening on a Saturday?

Pick it on Friday.

What do you get if you cross
a river with a giant gooseberry?

To the other side.

What do you get if you cross
a river with an ordinary gooseberry?

Wet.

**Why did the man have to go to hospital
after the gooseberry fell on his
head?**

It was in a tin.

What side of a gooseberry is the hairiest?

The outside.

What does a gooseberry do when it's raining?

Gets wet.

How do you make a gooseberry stew?

Keep it waiting for two hours.

What did the green gooseberry say
to the blue gooseberry?

'Cheer up!'

What's the difference between a
gooseberry and a worm?

Ever tried eating worm pie?

What's the difference between a
gooseberry and an elephant?

*Pick them up – an elephant is usually
heavier.*

What's green and hairy and
goes up and down?

A gooseberry in a lift.

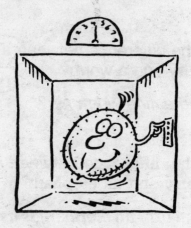

What did the gooseberry say
to the hungry maggot?

You're boring me.

What did the gooseberry say
to the greenfly?

You really bug me.

What do you call a two-ton
gooseberry with a nasty temper?

'Sir!'

What do you have when 2,000
gooseberries try to get through a door
together?

Gooseberry jam.

What do you get when you cross
a gooseberry with a chicken?

*A hen that lays green and hairy
eggs.*

Where do you find wild gooseberries?

It depends where they were lost.

If your cat ate an unripe gooseberry, what would she become?

A sourpuss.

What is green and hairy, has one bionic eye, and fights crime?

The Six-Million-Dollar Gooseberry.

Where do giant gooseberries come from?

Giant gooseberry bushes.

What is the best way to keep gooseberries?

Don't return them.

What's green and hairy and goes round and round?

A gooseberry in a spin.

What's enormous and yellow,
and says 'Fe-fi-fo-fum?'

A giant lemon.

What's yellow and goes slam,
slam, slam, slam?

A four-door lemon.

What's yellow, has four doors, and
goes beep, beep, beeeeeeeeep?

A lemon with a jammed horn.

How do you make a lemon drop?

Shake the tree hard.

What's
yellow
and goes
thump,
squish,
thump,
squish?

*A lemon
with
one
wet
plimsoll.*

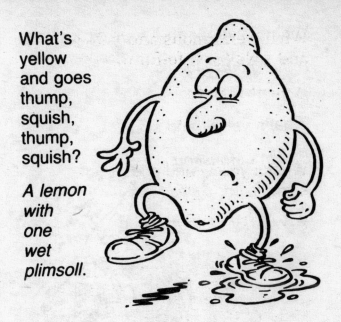

Why did Cinderella's fairy
godmother change the pumpkin
into a coach?

She didn't have a lemon handy.

What's yellow and goes click-click?

A ball-point banana.

What's yellow and sings?

Banana Mouskouri.

What's yellow on the inside and green on the outside?

A banana disguised as a cucumber.

What's yellow, wears a cape, and fights crime?

Superbanana.

What's yellow and hums?

An electric banana.

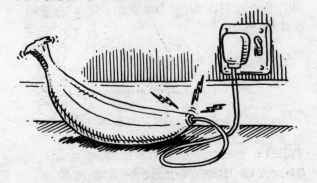

What's yellow and goes putt-putt?

An outboard banana.

Why is a banana skin like a
pullover?

They're both easy to slip on.

Why did the banana split?

Because it saw the apple turnover.

Why didn't the banana snore?

*Because it was afraid of waking up
the rest of the bunch.*

What did the boy banana say to the
girl banana?

'You appeal to me.'

Why don't bananas care what people
say about them?

Because they're thick-skinned.

Where should a twenty-pound
banana go?

On a diet.

What is the easiest way to make a banana split?

Cut it in half.

When an apple hits a banana, what is it called?

A fruit punch.

What's big and yellow and lives in Scotland?

The Loch Ness Banana.

What do
you do
with a
green
banana?

*Teach it
something.*

Teacher? If I cut two bananas and
two apples into ten pieces each, what
will I get?
Pupil: A fruit salad.

Why don't bananas have dandruff?

*Did you ever see a banana with
hair?*

What's yellow, washable, dries
quickly and doesn't need ironing?

A drip-dry banana.

What's green, covered in custard, and moans a lot?

Gooseberry grumble.

How can you tell when there's an elephant in your custard?

By the lumps.

What's yellow and can't count to 10?

Thick custard.

Did you hear about the man who stole some gooseberries?

He was put into custardy.

'Waiter, is there custard on the menu?'

'No sir, I wiped it off.'

A man saw a gardener pushing a wheel-barrow full of manure.
'Where are you going with that?' he asked.
'I'm going to put it on my gooseberries,' said the gardener.
'Suit yourself,' the man replied.
'I usually put custard on mine.'

What's yellow and highly dangerous?

Shark-infested custard.

What flies around the kitchen at
600mph and glows yellow?

An Unidentified Flying Omelette.

'Tough luck,' said the egg in the
monastery.
'Out of the frying-pan, into the
friar!'

Knock knock.
– *Who's there?*
Egbert.
– *Egbert who?*
Egbert no bacon.

What's yellow and white and travels at 90mph?
A train-driver's egg sandwich.

Why did the egg go into the jungle?
It was an eggsplorer.

If an egg came floating down the Mississippi River where would it have come from?
A chicken.

**What's white
and fluffy
and swings
from cake-shop
to cake-shop?**

A meringue-utang.

What's white and fluffy, has
whiskers, and floats?

A cata-meringue.

What is purple and crazy?

A grape nut.

What is a raisin?

A grape with a lot of worries.

What's round and purple
and bad at cooking?

Alfred the Grape.

What's big, purple and
lies in the sea?

Grape Britain.

What's purple and lives
in South America?

A Grape Train Robber.

What's purple and burns?

The Grape Fire of London.

What's purple and swings through the trees?

Tarzan of the Grapes.

What's purple and 4,000 miles long?

The Grape Wall of China.

What was purple and ruled the world?

Alexander the Grape.

What's purple and round and floats up in the sky?

The Planet of the Grapes.

What American lakes are filled with purple juice?

The Grape Lakes.

What did the grape say when the elephant trod on it?

Nothing – it just gave a little wine.

What sits in a fruit bowl
and shouts for help?

A damson in distress.

**Who was purple and discovered
America in 1492?**

Christopher Plumbus.

Which was the smallest plum?

Tom Plum.

Why does a plum make a good
museum-keeper?

Plum preserves.

What should you do if your
pet plum falls ill?

Call the plumber.

Who is purple, rides a motorbike,
and jumps over buses?

Evel Plumevel.

Why did the plum go into hospital?

He was plum crazy.

Why did the apple turnover?

Because it saw the Swiss roll.

Why wouldn't the man eat apples?

Because his granny had died of apple-plexy.

What animals in Noah's Ark didn't come in pairs?

Worms, they came in apples.

What do you call a Welsh apple?

Taffy apple.

'Mum, can I have some money for the old man crying outside in the street?'
'Of course, son. What's he crying about?'
'Toffee apples – for sale!'

Confucius, he say: An apple a day keeps the doctor away – if aimed correctly.

When is an apple not an apple?

When it is a crab.

Did Adam and Eve ever have a date?

No, they had an apple.

'What are you doing in my apple tree, young man?
'One of your apples fell down, sir, and I'm putting it back.'

What lives in apples and is an avid reader?

A bookworm.

What do you get when you cross an apple with a Christmas tree?

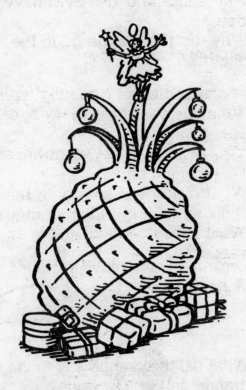

A pine-apple.

What do you get if you cross a citrus fruit with a bell?

An orange that can peal itself.

Why did the orange go to the doctor?

Because it wasn't peeling well.

What did one chick say to the other chick when it found an orange in the nest?

Look at the orange mama laid!

What did the orange say to the other orange on the telephone?

Nothing, the pips went.

Why couldn't the orange get up the hill?

Because it had run out of juice.

What does a vegetarian vampire eat?

Blood oranges.

What do you get when you cross an orange and a squash court?

Orange squash.

What do you do with a hurt lemon?

Give it lemon-aid.

What is a tangerine?

An orange in an easy-open wrapper.

What was the orange doing
in a palm tree?

*It had heard that coconuts
have more fun.*

Why are oranges and lemons
safe from pickpockets?

They don't have pockets.

What did one strawberry say to the other strawberry?

Between you and me, we shouldn't be in this jam.

What do farmers do to endangered strawberries?

Put them in preserves.

Did you hear the story about the world's biggest strawberry?

No.

Never mind, it's over your head.

How can you tell that strawberries are lazy?

They spend their entire lives in beds.

What is rhubarb?

Celery with high blood pressure.

What is red and wears a mask?

The Lone Raspberry.

What do you call an overweight pumpkin?

A plumpkin.

Why is history the sweetest lesson?

Because it's full of dates.

What's a good way of putting on weight?

Eat a peach, swallow the centre, and you've gained a stone.

What do you call a peach that is green and skinny at harvest time?

A failure.

What did the girl say after she ate a basket of fresh peaches?

'Burp!'

How were Humpty Dumpty and the peach with a weak stem alike?

They both had a great fall.

*   *   *

Why wouldn't the ripe peach sit on the wall?

It had heard what happened to Humpty Dumpty.

How do you tell a peach from a Jumbo jet?

A peach's tank is too small for it to cross the Atlantic without refuelling.

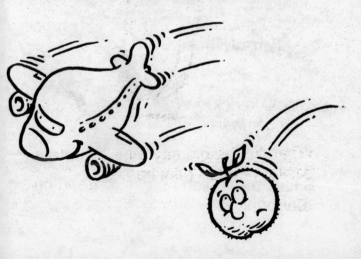

What is a prickly pear?

Two porcupines.

Knock, knock.
- *Who's there?*
Pear.
- *Pear who?*
Pair of shoes.

Knock, knock.
- *Who's there?*
Shoes.
- *Shoes who?*
Shoes me, I didn't mean to tread on your pear.

What do you call twins whose mother is a peach and whose father is a pear?

A peach of a pair.

What is the difference between a pear and an elephant?

A pear always forgets.

*   *   *

Why do pears always forget?

What do they have to remember?

**What's the biggest nut
in the British Army?**

The kernel.

**What nut sounds like
a sneeze?**

Cashew!

**Why did the peanut complain
to the police?**

Because he was a salted.

**How do you know peanuts are
fattening?**

*Have you ever seen a skinny
elephant?*

What nut has no shell?

A doughnut.

What do you call it when monkeys throw coconuts at each other?

Gorilla warfare!

Which nut invaded Britain?

William the Conker.

What's brown and chocolatey outside, has a peanut inside, and sings hymns?

A Sunday School Treet.

What's brown, woolly, covered in chocolate, and goes round the sun?

A Mars Baaaaaa!

Mother: There were two Mars bars in the larder yesterday, and now there's only one. Why?
Son: It must have been so dark I didn't see the other one.

What did the chocolate bar say to the lollipop?

Hi-ya, sucker!

What's brown and hairy, and bashful?

A coconut shy.

What's brown and hairy, and coughs?

A coconut with a bad chest.

What's brown, and eaten by French people for breakfast?

Huit heures bix.

How many cabbages can you put in an empty sack?

One. After that, the sack isn't empty.

Why didn't the boy eat his spinach after his mother told him it would put colour in his cheeks?

He didn't want green cheeks.

What sort of vegetables do plumbers fix?

Leeks.

What's the difference between mouldy lettuce and a dismal song?

One is a bad salad, and the other a sad ballad.

What do you call a vegetable's wages?

His celery.

Teacher (on school dinner duty): Any complaints?

Pupil: Yes sir, these peas are too hard.

Teacher (taking a spoonful and tasting them): They seem soft enough to me.

Pupil: They are now. I've been chewing them for the last half hour.

What grows in the garden and is a Kung Fu expert?

Bruce Leek.

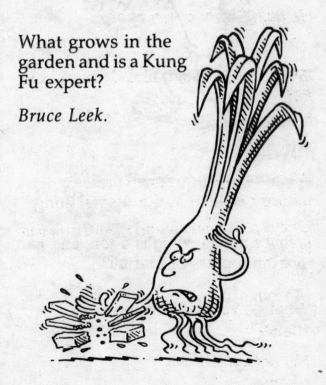

What's green and very fast?

A runner bean.

What's green, weighs a ton, and can float in a glass of Martini?

An olivephant.

What's green and plays snooker?

A cue-cumber.

What's big and green, has four legs, and if it fell out of a tree would kill you?

A snooker table.

What's the difference between a market gardener and a billiard-player?

One minds his peas, and the other minds his cues.

Why did the carrot colour itself green?

So it could hide in the cucumber patch.

*   *   *

Did you ever see a carrot in a cucumber patch?

See – the disguise worked.

What is the poorest plant?

A vine, because it cannot support itself.

What does a vegetarian cannibal eat?

Swedes.

What vegetable should you pick to go with jacket potatoes?

Button mushrooms.

What do you get if you cross rabbits with leeks?

Bunions.

Two ears of corn were running up a hill. What were they when they got to the top?

Puffed wheat.

How do you make jumping beans?

Go up behind them and shout 'Boo'!

What do you call two turnips who fall in love?

Swedehearts.

What is green, curly, and shy?

Lettuce alone.

What is green, curly, and goes around
at 100mph?

A Lettuce Elan.

What is green, curly, and religious?

Lettuce pray.

Why was the farmer cross?

Because someone trod on his corn.

Is it true that carrots are good for the eyesight?

Well, you never see rabbits wearing glasses.

How do you find a lost rabbit?

Make a noise like a big carrot.

What's long, orange and shoots rabbits?

A double-barrelled carrot.

Doctor, doctor, I've got carrots
growing out of my ears!
How on earth did that happen?
I don't know – I planted cucumbers.

Bert: Why do you have carrots
sticking out of your ears?
Fred: You'll have to talk louder. I have
carrots sticking out of my ears.

Why did the farmer run a steamroller over his potato patch?

Because he wanted mashed potatoes.

Did you hear about the farmer who planted his potatoes with razor blades in them? He wanted to grow chips.

How do you make a potato puff?

Chase it around the garden.

What do hedgehogs have for dinner?

Prickled onions.

What garden plant has eyes but never needs glasses?

The potato.

What do you get if you cross a potato with an onion?

A spud with watery eyes.

What happened to the potato that refused to work?

It was sacked.

Where do you find chilli beans?

At the North Pole.

How did the green cabbage talk to
the lettuce?

Head to head.

Why did the police arrest the green
cabbage?

It was involved in a garden plot.

Why was the green cabbage disliked
by all the other vegetables?

It had a big head.

How can you tell an apple from a
green cabbage?

If it's red it's probably an apple.

Knock, knock.
– *Who's there?*
Beets.
– *Beets who?*
Beets me, I just forgot the joke.

Knock, knock.
– *Who's there.*
Bean.
– *Bean who?*
Bean working hard lately.

Why did the grey elephant sit on the red tomato?

It wanted to play squash.

What's round, red and cheeky?

Tomato sauce.

What can a whole red tomato do but half a red tomato can't?

Look round.

Why did the tomato go red?

Because it saw the salad dressing.

Why was the red tomato in such a hurry?

It wanted to ketchup.

What is a vampire's favourite soup?

Scream of tomato.

What's green and holds up stage coaches?

Dick Gherkin.

What's short and green and goes camping?

A Boy Sprout.

What's green and goes boing-boing?

Spring cabbage.

What's green, seven feet tall, and mopes in the corner?

The Incredible Sulk.

*   *   *

What's green and wrinkled?

The Incredible Sulk's granny.

How do you make golden
vegetable soup?

Use fourteen carats.

There were two tomatoes on
horseback. Which was the cowboy?

Neither – they were both redskins.

Why shouldn't
you tell
secrets in
a vegetable
garden?

*Because corn
has ears,
and beans talk.*

What's orange
and comes out
of the ground
at 100mph?

*A jet-propelled
carrot.*

'Doctor, can you give me something
for my liver?'

'How about a pound of onions?'

How do you calculate the colour of a cabbage?

Use a green gauge.

What stands on one leg and has its heart in its head?

A cabbage.

What's the quickest way across the vegetable patch?

The dual cabbage-way.

What did the cabbage say when he knocked on the door?

'Lettuce in.'

Why are large cabbages generous?

Because they have big hearts.

What's green and round and points North?

A magnetic cabbage.

Baby Cabbage: Mummy, where did I come from?

Mummy Cabbage: The stalk brought you, dear.

What magazine do vegetable growers read?

The Weeder's Digest.

What's green and slimy and
is found at the North Pole?

A lost frog.

What's green and slimy and
highly dangerous?

A frog with a machine-gun.

What do frogs drink?

Croaka-Cola.

What's green with red spots?

A frog with measles.

What happens to a frog's car when it breaks down?

It gets toad away.

Where do frogs leave their coats at the theatre?

In the croakroom.

What ballet is most popular with frogs?

Swamp Lake.

What's white outside, green inside,
and hops?

A frog sandwich.

Where do frogs go when they've got
bad eyesight?

To a hoptician.

What do you call a girl with a frog on
her head?

Lily.

What do you call a frog spy?

A croak and dagger agent.

What's green and slimy and lives in a lighthouse?

A frog-horn.

What's green and slimy and red?

A frog with sunburn.

What is bright blue, weighs a ton, has four legs and talks?

Two half-ton parrots.

What colours would you paint
the sun and the wind?

The sun rose and the wind blew.

'That's a strange pair of socks you've
got on – one dark blue and one light
blue.'

*'I know – I've got another pair just
like it at home.'*

What's blue and yellow and has a
wingspan of 60 feet?

A three-ton budgie.

Have you any blue ties to match my
eyes?

*No, but we've got some soft hats to
match your head.*

What goes in green and comes out blue?

A gooseberry swimming on a cold day.

Why did the policeman wear indigo braces?

To keep his trousers up.

Sherlock Holmes: Ah, Watson, you are wearing your violet thermal underpants today . . .

Dr Watson: Absolutely astounding, Holmes! How on earth did you deduce that?

Sherlock Holmes: Elementary, my dear Watson. You forgot to put on your trousers.

What's blue and round and has eight wheels?

A blueberry on roller-skates.

I heard a good green and hairy joke and was going to take it home, but I decided that that was carrying a joke too far.